Diamond

Published by
Smugcat Media and Publishing
20 Poole Hill Bournemouth BH2 5PS
1st Edition 10 December 2017

Some Adult Content Strictly Over Eighteen

 Smugcat Media: Bournemouth

Dedication

This book is dedicated to all those women in my life who along the way have inspired these words.

PREFACE

Diamond In The Dark is my first foray into prose or poetry. That sounds if you're me, completely wrong! For someone who had a very sketchy education I find calling my writing Poetry or Prose disrespectful too much better writers than I! I like to call my writing, musings or wordoodles, as they just fall out the bottom of my pen! I like them and I write for me, so it's a bonus if anyone else connects with my words! They in reality are inspired by the women who have inhabited the inside of my head, or is it a woman? I will let the reader decide! So her they are, a selection of my wordoodles!

If you see by the title of a Wordoodle, Poem or piece of Prose the word EXPLICIT that is a warning it contains adult content!

Diamond in the Dark

There have been many women in my life.

Some only for a fleeting time.

Some for much longer, much longer than they should have been.

Some left with pain, much pain!

Some left with a sense of relief.

But in all my life, there has never been a woman who I could say; vibrated as I.

No woman, that I could get out of bed in the morning, look back at the sleeping deity, throw back the curtains look up to the heavens and say; 'thank you, God!'

No woman, until one night in the darkness, I saw a light.

Dimly at first, but getting steadily brighter.

A diamond was shining in the distance.

I reach for it, but it is too distant.

Intangible to touch.

Perspective all wrong, close but distant, the light dazzled me in the darkness.

Feeling the gems vibration.

Our frequencies aligned.

I reach for it, wanting to be close to it, to possess it, to cleave it from the rock.

But the diamond is always out of arms reach.

Panic now ensues, play it cool.

Let the jewel come to you.

What can I do?

Nothing!

There have been many women in my life.

But never a gem, a prize such as you!

The Wolf

In this season of fairy-tale and legend, he paints himself as almost a hero.

He imagines himself snatching the poisoned apple from the rose-red lips of the raven-haired princess with the snow-white skin and replacing it with an urgent kiss from his own hungry mouth.

He dreams of braving the vicious thorns of imprisoning briar to lift the unmoving but gorgeous living body of the sleeping beauty from out of her silent coffin. To carry her to some safe and secret place and wake her with the heat of his breath upon her barely pulsing, newly naked throat.

He sees himself placing the glass shoe on the delicate foot of the young, innocent, poorly treated servant girl and claiming her wide-eyed perfection, beauty, purity and love for always.

Yet the girl he really wants, the angel in the red hooded cloak, knows him as the dangerous creature of which her mother has warned. He is the restless stranger with poetry in his head, desire in his heart, and a world of darkness in his soul.

It is true that his teeth and claws can be sharp and he has such a decadent yet eloquent hunger.

But now, in these fading days and threadbare nights, even the wolf yearns only to be loved!

His Words

She sifts through his poems studying every nuance examining every subtext measuring every sentence considering every meaning reviewing every word.

She digs ever deeper for a fragment of her!

The Photograph

As I look at your photograph I imagine gently lifting your chin with the tips of my long fingers and placing a tender kiss in the perfect scented hollow of your elegant throat.

In my mind it is the first of a thousand more kisses to brush and touch and taste and caress over and over every single inch of your exquisite silken skin!

It will be you

When warm sun kisses my skin it will be you.

When cool breeze strokes my hair it will be you.

When velvet night holds me close it will be you.

Thinking of you

An evening
With good friends
Good wine
Good food
Good music
Yet I still found it hard
Not to think of you!

You Are

You are my last fantasy before I sleep.
My first fantasy when I awake.
And all of my wild and wicked dreams in between

Inclined and Ready

She has discovered him!

She has watched him, studied him, scrutinised him, reviewed him, analysed him!

She has surveyed him, evaluated him, interpreted him, and considered him!

She has pondered, reflected and deliberated!

She has read him carefully!

She has nervously sipped at the heady wine of his soft erotic words!

She has tasted them on her tongue, held them in her mouth, and felt them slide down her throat!

She has felt dizzy at the power of his prose, and the command his words demand!

She has begun to understand the nature and strength of her own self, her individual needs, her own desires!

She is ready for his seduction, his tutoring, to bathe in his syllables, as they caress her curves!

Feeling them penetrate her mind, losing control!

She is inclined; she is ready to be his!

I walk alone

I walk alone by the waterside a sad reflection on the water I see, like a dream that drifted away and then on the tide floats back to me.

For there's a love that's forever on my mind!

Just a man of too few summers with a love light in his eye, for the years that are between us I had no care. You said that I was foolish for our love was doomed to die, but still.

There's a love forever on my mind!

Photographs and letters of our times are just stories in my mind. I pray when the morning comes I'll leave it all behind.

Until then, there's a love forever on my mind.

When the storm clouds were are all around one cold March morning, and with words so hard to hear still ringing in my ear, you were gone without a warning!

So now again.

I walk alone by the waterside.

With a love, that's forever on my mind!

I will use you EXPLICIT

I will use you, every inch of you.

Your luscious skin, your gorgeous hair, your cheekbones, your eyes, your nose, your mouth. The elegant line of your jaw, your throat, your neck. Your sensual curves, the stunningly sexy shape of your breasts. Your nipples (so easily aroused).

Your back, your belly, your arse, your legs, your ankles, your calves, your thighs. Your arms, your hands, your fingers, your feet, your oh-so-prettily painted toes. The delicate, exquisite, flawless folds of your perfect sex.

I will use you.

The glorious curve of your smile. The joyful, soft peal of your laughter. The way you move, the way you eat, and the way you talk. The way you say my name. The way you dance. Oh god, the way you dance.

I will use you.

Your thoughts, your hopes, your dreams, your imagination. How you analyse, how you consider, how you (sometimes over) react. The way you care. Your honesty, your loyalty, your charity, your generosity, your charm. Your temper, your obstinance, your tenacity, your strength. Your sometimes stubborn frown. Your warmth. Your tears sliding hot and unchecked down your lovely face.

I will use you.

Your clothes, your shoes, your scent, your makeup, your jewellery. The toys you keep at the back of a bedside drawer.

Your music, your books, your art, your films. The (often rubbish) things you watch on TV. Your work, your hobbies, your interests, your exercise. How you spend your days. Your food, your drink, your wine. The things that excite you arouse you frighten you, sadden you, disturb you. The things that make you want to be hugged.

I will use you.

Every fantastic, challenging, beautiful, infuriating, incredible, shy, breath taking part of you. Everything that makes you, rare and unique.

I will use you.

And I will write you.

My heroine, my fantasy, my main protagonist, my crucial character. The star of the show. The woman at the very heart of it. And you alone, all by yourself, will make it magnificent.

You will turn my untidy jumble of words into a masterpiece!

An Autumn Sunday

Late sun sinking
Breeze blowing
Leaves falling
Incense burning
Music playing
My fingers
Idly tapping
The keyboard

A mug of Assam tea, close to hand.

You, in my head.

This truly is an Autumn Sunday for a writer!

My every sentence EXPLICIT

She lingers in my words sleek and smooth.

Silky and seductive, soft and sweet, a subtle, scented sensual shadow.

Her sheer sexual presence sculpts and shapes my every sentence.

Perhaps one day EXPLICIT

I have her beauty hard-wired into me!

I have known it forever.

My first schoolboy fantasies were of her. She has never changed. The same hair, eyes, mouth, chin, nose. The same height, weight, posture and stance. The same shoulders, breasts, hips, arse and thighs.

The same mix of swagger and vulnerability, of shyness and chatter, of independence and surrender, of contemplation and fun.

Her beauty is burned into my soul!

And I have found her and loved her.

Once, twice, even three times.

Almost, never!

I keep looking.

Although my time here is running out.

Perhaps one day!

Fading Romantic EXPLICIT

I am a fading romanticist, alpha male, with a dominant streak from a time before dominant became a cliché.

With a love of all things beautiful and a taste for the darkly sensual and erotically decadent.

A lover of music, food and wine, literature, theatre, film and art.

A writer. Though not a good one. Of novellas, short stories, songs and poetry. The written word is my joy and my curse.

I am tallish; my blond hair has long gone white, overweight, but athletic, fit even, with dark hazel eyes and sensitive, sensual hands.

I am neither handsome nor unattractive. I am a realistic dreamer, an idealistic pragmatist.

I am a sexually dominant yet patient and sensual lover, to please and pleasure my love is my primary objective, whether it physical or cerebral!

I adore intelligent, elegant, independent-minded, beautiful, sexually driven women.

Particularly those who have yet to release the ache in their soul?

I am not young. I am faded and fading still.

But if the music is playing, and the wine is good, and the stars are shining brightly in a soft velvet night sky, and the light falls on me just right; then you might see the man who could and can still, take your heart!

How

How could you
Have walked
Talked
Danced
Sung
Ate
Drank
Breathed
Worked
Smiled
Slept
Laughed
Loved
Existed

In this world without me somehow knowing of your presence?

The Tango EXPLICIT

My lips upon her breast, the soft flesh beneath my tongue.

My mouth surrounds her nipple, as it stiffens between my teeth.

I pull, the nipple, it hardens, as the areola crinkles and shrinks.

Now my mouth moves on, her breath becoming shallow. At the reality of her situation!

My tongue, my lips, kissing, nipping the soft tissue of her belly as I work towards my goal!

My hands now join the ballet of our lovemaking, encapturing her soft fleshy orb's as my fingers torment and torture her wanting nipples.

Her breathing becoming faster as my mouth sucks on the fatty tissue of her soft Môn's Pubis, my teeth pulling on the hair of her well-trimmed cuff.

Her body becoming flushed and her sinuses tight as we are both now entrenched in our fight.

My tongue starts to do a dance, a dance of delight, between the soft swollen folds of her sex! That now glistens in the soft moonlight.

Her legs widen, her breathing now rapid in the anticipation, of my tongues arrival at its goal!

Her body arches at the first flick as it caresses her swollen bud.

A moan, a groan spills from her lips as she feels the first wave of her coming climax!

It crests and subsides before the next wave rises, and crest's to ebb, only to build again.

As my eager tongue dances the tango with her throbbing clit, she feels the next wave of her impending orgasm rise, she gasps.

As this wave she knows will take her to the beach!

Gripping the sheets, my head now clamped between her thighs.

Her body shudders, letting out a primal moan as her orgasm arrives throbbing in head and bone.

Laying back in sweet sexual satisfaction a smile upon her lips, at the realisation.

I'm not done yet, not done by far! As my tongue starts to dance the tango once again!

The longest road home

I would take the longest road home, through the cities where there are crowds and lost souls and men with ugly smiles.

Over high, lonely mountains where the ice and snow chill the bone.

Across the cruellest seas where the waves climb high to claim me and to drag me to the depths.

Amidst the unexplored forests where the trees usher in the menacing, rustling dark.

Into the bleakest deserts where the angry wind hurls sand into my eyes to blind me.

I would take the longest road home............if it meant passing by your door!

I Wonder EXPLICIT

I Wonder

What is it like to be with her, part of her world, if only just one slice? Tasting her, savouring a crumb at a time!

Hearing her words, knowing her dreams?

What is like to be hers

What is it like to be closer, stroking her hair, holding her body close to mine

What is like to be there, to be inside

To feel her skin, parting her thighs

What is like, deep, immersed, she surrounding, squeezing the throb inside.

I Wonder?

The Initiation EXPLICIT

There are such special moments.

There is that gorgeous, delicious, delicate, exquisitely hung moment when he slowly tugs down the zip at the back of her strapless dress and begins to peel it from her like a warm, second skin!

He has already fastened the blindfold for the first time about her pretty head. He has run the sharp pinwheel so tenderly over the divine surface of her perfect face as lightly as a tingling feather, across her full, pouting lips. Her nerve endings are alive and electric with its touch!

He has already run his long, slender fingers through her hair, and caressed her beautiful bare shoulders and her elegant neck, easily coaxing a sweet rose flush to climb onto her throat.

He has already run his hands over her body through the sheer fabric of her dress, gliding over her curves, making her nipples harden and increasing the hungry heat between her parted thighs!

And now, at this holy stage as he started to unwrap her, he pauses and smiles. Shivers of raw, sensual, erotic expectation dances like a cool fire through his body.

He loves this moment. When she has given herself to him. When everything is to be discovered. Everything is possible, everything is to be done!

He lets the dress fall in a dark, perfumed circle at her stiletto-heeled feet.

Her initiation has begun!

A bleak summers day

June should be sunny and warm
but outside like my heart, its grey and bleak

no birds in the sky
raindrops running down my windows
trees bending to the will of the wind on this wet, windy summers day

dark grey clouds hang and fill the horizon
a storm is on its way
or is it already here?

Her Wish EXPLICIT

She wishes he would write something for her.

A fantasy of endless, velvet, star-filled skies.

Of a wild, round, luminous moon hanging like a silver lantern. Of a warm, perfumed breeze stroking her hair and tugging gently at her dress.

Of the distant strains of a yearning, lone violin fading and rising through the whispering trees.

Of his hands releasing the pale silk gown from her eloquent shoulders, and it running off her naked body like a caress and falling with a sigh at her feet.

Of her perfect, dangerous, wondrous curves laid out by him on a fresh, crisp white linen sheet. Of her arms and legs stretched wide. Of his tongue, his lips, his fingers over every inch of her tingling skin, upon her sensual mouth, her exquisite breasts, and her urgent, swollen, fragrant sex.

Of him filling her with pleasure, with joy, and with himself.

In every way.

She wishes he would write something for her.

Imagine me

Watching you, as you dress, and undress!

Imagine me, adoring every inch of you.

Seductive

She slips
through my defences
her silent infiltration
is smooth
with soft
sensual
sexy
silky
sleek
submissive
seduction!

Tortured with pleasure EXPLICIT

A cool, darkened room.

Outside the sun is blistering the wooden shutters. Narrow shafts of light sear between the wood, striping the walls and ceiling.

And streaming all over you.

They band your body, striping you cream and coffee coloured, you are naked, face up, on the white-sheeted bed.

You are stretched out in a star shape. Your wrists and ankles are secured to the four corners by ropes through steel D rings on sturdy black leather cuffs. The bindings permit little movement.

No matter how hard you tug and strain against them!

You have been here for almost an hour. Your buttocks propped on a pillow and I have caressed you, kissed you, licked you, and stroked you. I have nibbled you, kneaded you, and lightly scratched you. I have teased you with my pinwheel, with a soft brush, with a scarf of silk, and with my twelve-stranded flogger, trailed over your skin.

And with two of the dozen toys that I have carefully arranged on the oak bedside table.

I have my trusty wand in my right hand. It whirrs
rather noisily yet it is a faithful servant. I am applying it
expertly to your already swollen and glistening sex.

With my left hand, I am tugging and pinching your
hard-as-berry nipples. Your body is bucking and
arching, wanting to push away from the
wands relentless, dimpled, vibrating touch yet at the
same time you desire to thrust yourself onto it.

Your breathing is urgent and hard. You are panting
and crying, sighing and moaning. I know you are
desperate to speak, to shout something at me. But you do
not. Your ecstasy has stuck you dumb.

Your body is dancing now. Strands of your hair are
damp and clinging with perspiration. Your face is
suffused and flushed with deep arousal. Your eyes roll
back. Your mouth is open.

Your muscles tighten. You shudder. The
orgasm reverberates through you!

It is your third climax!

The toy continues to send spasms through your body.
You make small noises of protestation. I smile. After a
while, I switch it off and idly but dangerously trail my
fingers over your inner thighs.

I consider which device to use next.

Later I will reposition you face down.

Later still I will fuck you! The way you want!

I have all afternoon ahead of me to torture you with pleasure!

The Show EXPLICIT

She is not shy. She has done this before. But not with a man like him!

She has rehearsed it so often that the music has become a soundtrack to these last few nervous days.

It plays in her mind from the moment sleep releases her until she slides back into its arms.

Perhaps it echoes through her dreams. She knows every persistent drumbeat, every smooth chord, every deep bass note, and every sweet moan of hungry, dirty brass. She has her timings to the second.

She has tried to imagine this moment, wanted to prepare herself for how she would feel.

Now, standing before him, she realises that she could never have readied herself. Not for this intimate space, this hushed room, this audience of one.

Her mouth is dry, her heartbeat is wild and loud, her legs are weak.

She is finding it hard to breathe.

She smooth's her hands down her dress. They slide over her waist and onto her hips. She is desperately nervous. She is blushingly embarrassed.

She is impossibly excited.

She is achingly aroused.

His eyes lock onto hers, and he smiles. He presses a button on the slim, black remote and the music begins. The first notes are soothingly familiar and disturbingly erotic.

Despite herself, she begins to sway into her routine. She feels her hips move. As if by magic her body becomes lithe and sinuous.

She is seductive, sexy, and sensuous!

He nods almost imperceptibly but somehow appreciatively.

Her hands glide over her breasts, caressing herself. Her fingers reach behind for the metal tongue of the zipper.

The show has begun!

Performance

She is performance
Potent
Proud
Physical
Powerful
Profane
Passionate
Precious
Pleasing
Persuasive
Provocative
Phenomenal
Perfect.

She is performance but purely for me!

Vanilla

There was a time
when I only liked
vanilla!

Since knowing you
my tastes
have changed!

I've been to see my doctor

My doctor has examined me

He is a man of great learning and deep understanding. He is old and wise, and the certificates on his wall attest to his vast and eclectic knowledge. Anatomy, psychiatry, psychology, neurology, surgery, geometry, chemistry, philately, campanology.

He took deep soundings from my pulse. He listened carefully to my heart. He examined my body with talented hands, the strength of my muscles, the structure of my bones, the conductivity of my nerves, the light in my eyes. He considered tendons, ligaments, and cartilage.

He had me listen to faint sounds. He made me recall half-forgotten scents. He insisted I recite my darkest poetry. He made my reflexes dance.

He asked me questions, recovered my dreams, investigated my hopes, and pondered over my expectations. Asked pointedly about my exercise, and my patterns of sleep. He explored my diet, my sexual inclinations, my sensual desires. My abuse of Assam tea and of course alcohol.

When he was done, he sat me down and faced me. His brow was furrowed, his mouth severe. His chin was set firm. He was serious in his approach. He was careful in his diagnosis. He shook his head sorrowfully, and with his fat fountain pen wrote slowly upon his pad.

He solemnly handed me the page.

He is a man of considerable reputation. I trust him completely. My doctor has examined me.

My doctor knows what ails me. He knows what has laid me low.

He is confident of the only thing that can make me well. His recommendation is precise and unequivocal.

My doctor has prescribed me you!

It is a repeat prescription.

Of unlimited dose.

To be taken as often as I require.

You

You move through my day

Like a sigh
Like a breath
Like a whisper
Like warm air
Like a soft breeze
Like a wild wind
Like a sea storm
Like a tempest
Like a hurricane

And I am blown away by all of them.

Your Skin

Thursday evening with a glass of the Irish!

My fingers caressing words from this keyboard!

Wishing they were stroking sighs from your skin!

Extraordinary

There are those of us
perhaps like you
and certainly like me
who live our lives
wanting something
more
something dark
and decadent
something wild
and beautiful
something exotic
erotic
and mysterious
something extraordinary!

Every Millimetre EXPLICIT

I sense you!

I feel your warmth, hear your breathing!

I catch a hint of your scent! I can almost taste your skin!

Your presence seems close.

Sensual, delicate, compelling, heavenly.

I imagine touching your face, your throat, your naked shoulders, and your exquisite breasts!

Belonging to you!

The thought thrills me beyond measure!

I want to know you entirely!

Every word, every breath, every smile, every sigh, every fantasy, every curve!

Every millimetre of your perfect body.

Tangled EXPLICIT

Oh to be there
tangled
in those sheets
your back pressed
against my chest
my hands
cupping your breasts
my face buried
in the storm
of your hair
inhaling deep
and overdosing
on the heady scent
of you!

Tomorrow

The best thing
about tomorrow
is that it is still
unwritten.

We may write it
mark it
draw it
paint it
stain it
brand it
fashion it
carve it
colour it
and give life to it
as we wish!

Trail of Kisses

I will trail
a shiver
of soft kisses
from ear to mouth
nape to throat
collar to breast
belly to hip
thighs to lips
breathing in
your scent
tasting the exquisite
and delicious desire
on your skin!

All Time

If only my love
I could take giant strides across
the land and sea
the mountain and streams
the forest and tundra
the snow and desert
swallowing distance
shrinking miles
eating the geography that's between us

I would come to claim your beauty, body
and soul!

For now and all time!

It may never come again

The things you do not do
when an opportunity arises
you will never do.

Because similar opportunities
are never quite the same
and the original opportunity
will never come again!

My Woman

She is the woman
who thinks
she might be pretty
but who everyone knows
is beautiful!

She is the girl
who dresses modestly
but still manages
to turn heads!

She is the girl
hidden in shadows
who everyone
cannot help
but notice!

She is the girl
who everyone knows
is always good
and could never be wicked!

She is the girl
who no one will guess
beneath her dress
that perfect body
she has given to me!

I would surely fall EXPLICIT

I have never met her.

Yet I can smell her scent on my fingers.

I can hear her laughter.

The way her voice lifts and dances and makes me smile.

I can feel the press of her body, her skin soft against mine, my face buried in her hair, I can imagine how she responds to my touch, the blush in her throat, the quickening of her breath and the rising of her breasts.

The hardening of her nipples!
Her wetness against my thigh!

I can taste her kiss. So intensely that I am running the tip of my tongue over my lips to capture the sweetness!

I can see her eyes, bright, eloquent, shining, luminous.

Making me sigh.

I have never met her, but if I did.

I would surely fall!

Think of Me EXPLICIT

Think of me
as a poet
a priest
a professor

Think of me
as a stranger
a shaman
a sorcerer

Think of me
as a doctor
a dancer
a disciple.

Use me
as the fantasy
who makes you blush
as you part your thighs
and arch your back
with your hand moving lower
when you are alone.

It so does

His dark
decadent
religion
should not
excite her
arouse her
thrill her
in any way
shape or form!

But it does
erotically
disturbingly
deliciously
exquisitely!

It should not, but it does!

Roadster

You have such
elegant
sleek
slender
stylish
svelte
pure
perfect
classy
classic
sports car
curves.

Driving you
would be
a delight!

It's the way it is EXPLICIT

 It is the nature
of his dark
BDSM religion.

His to direct
hers to serve.

His to teach
hers to learn.

His to own
hers to belong.

Theirs to adore
and be adored.

Too many summers EXPLICIT

She has seen too many summers to be completely innocent.

And yet he has made her so.

She is new, pristine, and spotless.
She is pure, virtuous, chaste and naive.
She is unsullied, unblemished, undefiled.
She has become a neophyte, a learner, and a beginner.

A novice on her first day, her white dress pressed and spotless, the hem gently brushing her bare legs!

She is his pupil, his student, his apprentice, and his initiate.

She is his disciple, his follower, and his protégé.
She is his love, his angel, his goddess, and his muse!

In this quiet, holy, secret place, she kneels before him.

Her mind and body are burning.

She is ablaze with desire.
She is thirsty for knowledge.
She aches to learn every rule, every code, every facet, every element, and every shade.

Every verse of his dark and decadent religion.

She is hungry for him to instruct her, to teach her, to guide her!

To show her a wild, breathless universe of pleasure and sensation!

Exquisite anticipation to complement his exquisite touch!

She wants him to do everything!

And at this moment she is his to do with, as he will!

The sheets caress EXPLICIT

Sometimes as she lies in bed
she is so taut with desire
that the touch and caress
of the cotton sheet
brushing against her naked skin
causes her to catch her breath
bite her lip and slide her hands
between her aching thighs!

That are now yearning for release!

Separate and different

In their separate
different
distinct
distant
unconnected
lives
they both wished
for something
for someone
special!

On meeting
across the miles
by chance
by coincidence
by serendipity
they both discovered
they had wished
for each other!

Billions

So many billions of souls
milling around!

in confusion
in frustration
in desolation
in isolation
in depression
in anticipation
in expectation
in hope

On this relentlessly
spinning planet.

Somehow ours collided!

The thought of you

I adore the thought of you
dressing getting ready
to meet me
hot water running
in rapid rivers
your skin slick
with scented soap
blushing with heat
and anticipation!

I adore the thought
of you
getting ready
lazily lingering
in lacy lingerie
sexily slipping
into silky stockings
sleek and sensual
in a sheath of a dress!

I adore the thought
of you
getting ready
pristine, painted
poised and peerless
perfectly prepared
for our night.

Cunnilingus EXPLICIT

Pressing her legs wide, lips on inner thighs glide! A waft of excitement, such heady enticement!

Raising up her thighs, so on my shoulders lies! Just inches away, bending forward to play!

My lips press to hers, tender pleasure confers! Nibbling fat outer lips, spreading with fingertips!

Sucking pink inner ones, as her sleek nectar runs! Pushing tongue inside, soft groans she cannot hide!

My head grabbing for, as she implores for more! Tongue pressing deeply in, juices running down chin!

Lapping them up, searching for more to sup! Thighs holding me tighter, as she bucks in rapture!

Drinking juice that flows, until her trembling slows!

A brief lapse

It only takes
a brief lapse
of my concentration
a soft slide
into a daydream
a sudden shift
into my imagination
an easy glide
into meditation
an idle fall
into fantasy
and I am lost
in a world
of only you!

Afar

You are a distant land

One I will never reach. Never touch. Never fully claim.

And yet I want to know your geography.
Every inch of your tempting, tender terrain.
I want to uncover your lovely, luscious landscape.
Study you from each perfect, precious, peerless, perspective.

Map your marks, covet your curves, lust over your lines, ache for your angles.

I want to discover you.
I want to uncover you.
And cover you with words.

I want to be thrilled by my journey to the very heart of you.

Adoring you
Wanting you
Worshipping you

From afar

Devotion

His love
ignores borders
crosses continents
skims over oceans
skips over mountains
defies distance to
claim her, the one he loves!

His devotion
is not everything
she wants
or needs
but oh god
it turns her on so!

No Compromise

Your beauty
maybe luminous
your intellect
formidable
your body
immaculate
your wit
wonderful
your sensuality
eloquent
your seduction
exquisite
your creativity
compelling

Yet I will never
compromise!

I'm my own man
It's the person I am!

My Love

You know
you have
been my love
in a hundred
hidden pasts.

You will
be my love
in countless futures
to come.

You are my love
now and in infinite time!

Safe

When the world
is torn by conflict
starved by greed
betrayed by belief
brutal with hate
it is enough to know
that you,
my angel,
are safe.

A different sort of cat

He was sleek a different breed of cat, slow-paced pleasant, admirably laid back!

And, it took years to find this kind of passion and dedication in one, from what all, the others lacked!

He meandered gracefully, through crowds of beauty, his held powerful gaze, softened to show off the deepest dimples as he smiled!

Regal natured like a King.

A man of his word, with sufficient intelligence, and eyes that sung.

Most sat by imagining having a fling, they were astonished by his honesty, most intrigued by his compliments, for they meant, everything!

So fair was his look and athletic his physique, one gaze into his eyes left ones heart so weak!

I grew more fascinated by his prince charming stare, for I'd caught a glimpse of him seeking me out, his eyes whispering too care!

So enraptured by his aura, I became motivated to take on a personal dare! Talking and laughing with him until he measured the distance of my heart and found it fair!

For, he was a different kind of cat, one that raised curiosity's hair on the back of my neck, as he roared promises of passion!

Yes, a very different kind of cat and in my eyes, I was assured his attention would never slack!

Fantasy

Suddenly
she realises that
her pulse was racing
her heart was pounding
her mouth was dry, so very dry
her thoughts tumble in her head
over themselves so dangerously!

In the realisation that she
is the one he wants!

She is his fantasy!

And Then

I thought I had become immune to beauty!

indifferent to sexy

unmoved by surrender

unstirred by intelligence

unexcited by control

untouched by desire

unaffected by dance

And then there was you!

Drenched

This rain will never end.

It hurtles towards the ground in urgent lines of hissing, insistent, driving, silver sorrow. The swollen sky is fat with threatening thunder and lit by livid flashes of ill-tempered lightning.

The pious are building desperate arks amongst the sodden ruins of their bruised, spoiled, pointless summer. The makeup on the faces of the carnival children is streaked and sad.

The hair on the pretty girls is hanging lank and wet on their white-skinned shoulders; their cotton dresses are clinging to their sun-starved legs. Boys without purpose suck on damp cigarettes and watch the flood from beneath noisy, dripping, green trees.

I will drink my red wine and imagine myself beneath a friendly blue sky where the sun is hot and constant and where the sea gently nudges the fishing boats as they rest for the day.

I will try not to let this miserable, grey, tiresome beast of depression that the cruel rain has ushered in wrestle me down into muddy brown puddles of chilly despair.

I will try, but as the feeble evening light seeps into the greyness, I can already feel its dark, slippery, familiar weight descending upon me. Drowning me in its dreariness!

Plunder

Tonight
when I dream
of paradise
there will be pirates
and thieves
full sails
and deep seas
tall ships
and mutiny
adventure
and destiny.

Tonight
when I dream
of paradise
you will be
my treasure
and
my plunder!

Rags and Teddy

Once upon a time through a door just down the hall in a dark, forgotten corner of the playroom was a doll.

She was only made of cloth, a rather simple work of art, but you could see where someone had embroidered her a heart.

It had faded from neglect and being lonely through the years, she couldn't even cry because she hadn't any tears.

But then one day as she lay cold and silent on the floor, a teddy bear was tossed in through the squeaky playroom door.

As she watched him, he got to his feet and slowly walked her way; her little red embroidered heart came to life that very day.

He gently picked her up, and as he held her in his arms, he noticed a faint heartbeat and certain rag doll charms.

So he took some thread and stitched a pretty twinkle in her eye and fixed her sewed-on smile, which had long-since gone awry.

He brushed away the dust and cobwebs from her dress then taught her about love in his fuzzy warm caress.

Those two have stayed together since that day so long ago; and when he looks at her today, he would hardly even know.

That this happy little rag doll so content and satisfied, was the same one he had found cast so carelessly aside!

Filling my summer

The days have lengthened out,
warbled from the first stirrings
of tireless birds woken by the dawn
to the dark shapes of bats,
soundlessly haunting the dusk.

My body has stretched out,
relaxed by the light-filled hours,
touched warm by the sun's rays
and moving effortlessly to the music
of you filling my summer days!

If I Could

If I could wish
a hot summer
and you
bare-legged
short dress
high heels
cool room
brass bed
white sheets
hair wild
body mine
then I would

Right now and for always!

There comes a day

There comes a day, somewhere in the middle of every person's life, when Mother Nature herself stands behind us and wraps her arms around our shoulders, whispering

'It's time.'

'You have taken enough now. It's time to stop growing up, stop growing older and start growing wiser and wilder.

There are adventures still waiting for you and this time, you will enjoy them with the vision of wisdom and the companionship of hindsight, and you will really let go.

It's time to stop the madness of comparison and the ridicule of schedule and conformity and start experiencing the joys that a life, free of containment and guilt, can bring.'

She will shake your shoulders gently and remind you that you've done your bit. You've given too much, cared too much, you've suffered enough.

You've bought the book, as it were, and worn the t-shirt.

Worse, you've worn the chains and carried the weight of a burden far too heavy for your shoulders.

'It's time' she will say.

'Let it go, really let it go and feel the freedom of the fresh, clean spaces within you. Fill them with discovery, love and laughter. Fill yourself so full you will no longer fear what is ahead and instead, you will greet each day with the excitement of a child.'

She will remind you that if you choose to stop caring what other people think of you and instead care what you think of you, you will experience a new era of your life you never dreamed possible.

'It's time' she will say...

'To write the ending, or new beginning, of your own story.'

Satisfied

I am satisfied

when a sense of you

runs through my day

like a golden thread

like a pulse of desire

like the scent of musk

like the warm sun on my back

like the taste of fine red wine

like the most touching lines

from my favourite song!

Rhythm of Need

There is music
between them
a cadence
a pulse
a beat
that resonates
across the miles
across the borders
across the mountains
across the seas.

A harmony of longing
a rhythm of desire
a duet of need!

Her Priest

Sometimes she thinks he is a priest.

Or a professor, or a doctor, or a therapist.

Sometimes she thinks he is a teacher
or a shaman, or a philosopher, or a guide.

But sometimes she thinks he is a gardener!

Carefully sowing a decadent seed of a dark idea or a
dangerous desire.

That takes root wickedly and grows wildly and
endlessly inside her until she can think of nothing else!

No Limits

I impose
no limits
or boundaries
or morals
or principles
or controls
or moderation
or suppression
or inhibition
or restrictions
or restraints
on my subconscious mind
when it dreams
of you!

Your Illumination

I did not discover you
or devise you
or reveal you.

You already illuminate
your own life
and time.

But I captivated you
and admired you
and adored you
to bring your light
into mine.

Rain Dance EXPLICIT

I imagine you dancing naked in the summer rain.

I am jealous of the water, running in bold, sensual, certain rivers over every curve, every line, and every gorgeous inch of your flawless skin.

I am jealous of how it clings to you, caresses you, makes you shine like a goddess.

And yet I am also so impossibly thirsty for it. I am a parched man in a hot desert of desperate desire.

I want to drink it, to lick it, to suck it up, to gulp it down, to imbibe it, to consume it, to swallow it.

And to taste you in every single delicious drop!

Her Hands

She has let her hands
wander all over
her body
as if they belonged
to a lover
to a writer
to a teacher
to a priest
to an angel
to the devil
to her master.

As if they belonged
to a stranger.

As if they belonged
to me!

You turn me on

Who can explain
attraction
admiration
connection
appeal
fascination
infatuation
enchantment
desire
captivation
temptation
seduction
lust!

Who can explain
the magnetism
that draws me close?

Who can explain
any of it?

I just know
you turn me on!

Wait for the one

Wait for the one who simply adores you.

The person who brings out the best in you and makes you want to be a better person!

The only person who will drop everything to be with you at any time no matter what the circumstances, for the person who makes you smile like no one else ever has!

Wait for the person who wants to show you off to the world because they are so proud of you.

And most of all wait for the person who will make you a priority because that's where you belong!

Wow

Sometimes
I search through all my words
considering each for suitability
trying to find one
specific, precise, perfect
fit for purpose
that captures my emotion
provides description
yields illumination
offers reflection
delivers perspective
but when it comes
to you
all I can say is.......

WOW!

Seize the Day!

These brave and uncharted days
hold a perfect promise.

of such delicious, decadent discovery
of such sheer sensual satisfaction
of such thrilling fulfilment of fantasy
of such wild abandon
of such unburdened joy

Let us surrender to their sensual rhythm.

Let us give ourselves up to the magic of their
moments.

Let us yield to the endless ache within.

For you and I my beautiful friend.

Will never, ever pass this way again!

Your Scent

Somehow
across the miles
I catch
your distant scent
and imagine you
close
your movements
your breathing
your laughter
your eyes
shining
the silk of your hair
the taste
of your warm skin
against my lips!

The Rose

The red rose whispers of passion and sensuous stimulation!

The white rose breathes with love and lust.

I send you a cream-white rosebud, with a flush on its petal tips.

For the love that is sweet, as a kiss of desire on the lips

Like no one before EXPLICIT

I want my poetry
to seduce you
to undress you
to restrain you
to control you
to direct you
to pleasure you
to thrill you
to captivate you.

I want to love you
like no one before!

Something Important

I was going to write something important, relevant,
meaningful and deep!

Something incisive, prophetic, intuitive and bold!

Something intelligent, articulate, perceptive and wise!

Something that would make you see me
in a different light!

But all I can think about is removing your clothes!

An ordinary life

You may have had
an ordinary day
wearing ordinary clothes
doing ordinary things
with ordinary people
in an ordinary place
in an ordinary way
but you are certainly
not an ordinary girl.

You are an extraordinary Woman!

Dark Secret EXPLICIT

They share a secret.

A delicious, dirty, decadent secret.

It dances dangerously between them.

It is desperately dreamy with adoration.

It is dark with discipline, direction and dominance.

It is delicate, delightful and deep.

It drips with desire!

Encore EXPLICIT

I love to watch you touch yourself, on any given afternoon.

The wandering hands!

The soft little moans!

Hips twitching, writhing on the now damp white sheets!

Wet fingers sliding along your wanting slit!

A solo performance, performed for one!

Just being you

A day of blue
and gold
of cotton wool clouds
fluttering butterflies
insects whirring
bees buzzing
liquid birdsong
a caressing breeze
and the magical thought
of you
somewhere
just being you!

When the world conspires against you

I am here
when the world conspires
against you.

I am here
on your side
without judgement
without reservation
without qualification
without criticism
without presumption
without disapproval
without condemnation

I am here
on your side.

I am here
when the world
conspires against you.

On and On

There's a pain that goes on and on!

It's riven my heart and my soul
the hurt goes on and on.

It's in my head stuck in my brain
the pain the hurt goes on and on.

To know people you love
feel such enmity against you
there's a scream that goes on and on.

The woman, my love, I love so deeply
with a love that was meant to go on and on.

Why does she support this enmity?

Do nothing to support the man she loves
that is a question that goes on and on?

I do not

I do not make wishes
I do not cast spells
I do not pray
I do not practice
hypnosis.

I do not coerce
I do not threaten
I do not seduce
I do not bear gifts
to win you over.

I do not make deals
with the devil.

But I will, if I must because I do

Oh, I do want you!

Change Me

You might
charm me
seduce me
engage me

You might
excite me
enchant me
delight me

You might
thrill me
bewitch me
amaze me

You might
inspire me
arouse me
inflame me.

But you will
never ever
change me!

Approval

She studies herself in the full-length mirror.

She knows that he cannot see her, does not see her, may never see her!

Yet she turns through three hundred and sixty degrees, aware of her breasts beneath the shirt, her arse and her thighs, tight in her jeans, the way the morning light dances on her skin!

She runs her hands through her hair and lets it fall!

She hopes he likes the way she looks!

Although his eyes may never fall upon her, she still seeks his approval!

A Dark Place EXPLICIT

She is naked.

She runs her fingertips along her cheeks and lightly over lips.

So gently that her skin tingles!

She closes her eyes and trails them over her chin, onto her neck and into the hollow of her throat.

They trace a line across her collarbones.

She shivers.

But she is not cold.

She is surprised to find her skin so sensitive to her own touch.

She parts her thighs.

Wide.

As wide as she can!

Breathing hard she allows her hands to slide down and cup her breasts.

She slowly circles her areolae with her thumbs, feeling the already erect nipples harden into tight buds.

She strokes herself, exquisite arcs of excitement. She almost becomes lost in the sensation.

She imagines her hands becoming his. She is under his instruction, under his control.

She takes each nipple between thumb and forefinger.

She begins to squeeze.

Hard.

In her mind, she can hear his voice. Soft, deep, dark, commanding, specific!

'Harder'

She tightens her grip and gasps at the pain. And yet also the pleasure!

She knows she is wet.

Very!

His voice again!

'Harder'

This time she is brutal with herself. She cries out, yet maintains her vice-like grip.

It is like two electric shocks. Red-hot wires running from breasts to belly to sex.

Urgent, sharp, shocking!

Intense.

Heavenly.

The deep pitch of her arousal takes her breath away.

She realises her fantasies have suddenly taken her to a darker place!

Addiction

The uncaring night will take me
and oppress me with its heat.
Leave me wide-eyed
and sleepless in a tangle of tortured sheets.

Since you became my addiction
I have wanted no one else.
Only to see you dance before me
I have longed for nothing else.

The over-bright dawn will find me
and burden me with its hope.
Leave me confused and restless
tied up tightly in my own rope.

Since you became my addiction
I have wanted no one else.
Only to see you dance before me
I have longed for nothing else.

The relentless day will trap me
and unsight me with its glare.
Leave me wandering and helpless
your distance has stripped me bare.

Since you became my addiction
I have wanted no one else.
Only to see you dance before me
I have longed for nothing else.

More than your name

I whispered more than your name last night before
finally, I slept.

I whispered more than your name last night,
bravely into the dark, like a poem like a prayer!

I whispered more than your name last night,
hoping the soft seeking syllables, the wishing
wanting words would somehow reach you and touch
you deeply.

I whispered more than your name last night.

Perhaps you didn't hear!

A Selfie (Only for him)

The camera's eye blinks
the silent shutter
closing on her image
capturing it perfectly
a paradise of lines and curves
a heaven of hair and skin
a rapture of pure arousal
posed only for him!

It Hurts EXPLICIT

I want you in ways I have written a thousand times!

And yet make me hard when I apply them to you.

I want you in countless, endless fantasies, stacked in towers of gorgeous film reels in the dark corners of my mind!

I want you in visions of breath taking pleasure and exquisite pain, stripped and tied and teased and touched and tortured and adored!

I want you so fucking much it hurts!

Days

There will always be,
good days
bad days
joyful days
sad days
wild days
dark days
quiet days
golden days.

But they will never, be the same, as the days, spent with you!

I have been high

On the bottle, the rich taste of red wine in my mouth! Blackberry, cinnamon, nutmeg and leather!

Another glass and another follow!

And perhaps another!

Until all I know is crimson liquid!

Then Jameson & Ice or maybe Conker Gin, or Absinthe! To follow!

Or all three!

Pour me into a taxi and take me home!

I have been high on acid, once! Pills, blotting paper, microdots with happy, hippy names, in my youth!

Colours bleeding into surfaces into shapes into light!

Music holy with new tones and textures to touch! The revelations, the meanings, the weird, finding a new religion in a carpet.

The warm fade and glow of coming down.

I have been high on adventure, on exploration, on discovery, the new, the different, the strange, the erotic, the pain!

On art, on words, on music, on performance, on poetry! On the strings of my guitar, on her!

On winning, on deals, on negotiation. On a high-five finish!

On landscapes, seascapes, lucky escapes, and there's been a few!

On the lights on the harbour twinkling like diamonds!

On snow, on ice, on powder!

On that feeling, at the end of the page when everything is perfect!

I have had a lifetime of highs but nothing absolutely nothing, not a single thing comes close to the high you take me to!

She is sure

There is an intensity.

A wild, glorious, delicious dynamic that sings and hums through every communication! It sparks and crackles across the ether, vibrant, luminous, electric, and vital. It radiates heat, it scatters stars, and it shivers in the air like a lightning storm.

She can feel it dancing beneath her skin. It makes her nervous, elated, hungry. It fills her body with sensations that are new, exotic, dark, compelling, and urgent. She is drawn to him as if metal to a magnet.

He has released something inside her that constricts her throat and curls in her lower belly a constant yearning for something she has not yet discovered.

She is sure he wants her.

Naked

Images of naked strangers leave me cold!

Nudity has become far too common a currency to attract my attention or pique my interest.

A body is a body. Some are more elegant than others. Some have been treated better or worse by time. Some are cared for. Some are toned by exercise. Some are a paradise of lines and curves.

Some are the shape I admire.

But they do not raise my pulse.

Not unless I am attracted by the personality within.

By the intellect, the sense of humour, the creativity, the warmth.

The body, especially one without exclusivity after having been viewed by many, is merely a shell.

It is she who inhabits the body that gives it attraction, magic, desirability, and potency.

She gives it power!

The Morning EXPLICIT

Light is just beginning to seep into my room. It gives shape to furniture, illuminates pictures on the walls, and faintly smears a trace of gold onto my bed.

Outside stirring birds are beginning to sing themselves awake with liquid voices.

I glance at the time on my phone. I do not check for mail although I desperately want to.

But it is early. And anyway, messages will keep me awake.

I hope that you have written. But I know I'll be disappointed!

I feel my body stir, and my heart yearns, and I bury my head in the pillows with a sigh.

I begin to slide back into sleep.

You are not there, but I feel you next to me.

The heat of you!
The scent of you!

Your skin is soft against my mine. I feel your back against my chest. The perfect peach of your arse pressed against my growing erection. Your breasts held in my hands. Nipples hardening into my palms!

You whisper something soft and beautiful, but I hardly catch the words.

I feel you dissolving into me.

We are floating away.

My alarm sounds urgently.

My day begins.

You're gone!

Embrace

Perhaps we will meet
between night and day
physical and virtual
past and future
earth and heaven
dreams and reality
to become one
fused in the heat
of a timeless embrace!

A girl like you

In my youth, I would have fought other boys for the right to walk you home.

Wearing the scars like a badge.

Or I would have wandered backwards and forwards past your house, hoping to catch a glimpse of you at a window.

Or long for you to see me, a shadowy figure beneath the streetlight, and think me romantic.

In my youth, I would have carved presumptuous initials into innocent trees, into battered park benches, into tables, and desks, and the backs of chairs not caring if I was caught.

Or that you would disapprove if you knew!

In my youth I would have sought you out at dances, making a mess of my over rehearsed lines. I would have asked a friend to give you messages, which you would probably receive with a frown.

In my youth, I would have made up a hundred heroic stories in my head where I come to your rescue. Saving you from the clutches of the mob, the grip of an assailant, the jaws of death.

Or perhaps just finding your lost dog!

In my youth, I would have written you tortured poems, toiled over for hours, scrawled on stolen paper that would never leave the pocket of my faded denim jeans.

In my youth, I would have wished for the Internet, if I could have seen into the future.

Yet here I am.
Internet at my fingertips.
Posting pointless poetry.
To a girl like you!

Yours to give

In this season of giving and regeneration,
it is not mine to take.

It is not mine to demand, to request, to ask for, to seek.

It is not mine to solicit, to court, to appeal for, to beg.

It is not mine to insist, to cajole, and to call for, or to press.

It is not mine to neither petition for, steal nor propose.

It is yours to give!

Taken EXPLICIT

Backed up against the wall, hands the buttocks grab, easily lifting!

Trying to hang onto the neck, slipping down upon the thick shaft.

I'm impaled!

Filled with such hardness, thrusts bouncing me up and down flesh slapping loudly!

Taking me with such passion, forcefully sating my need!

Losing track of time nails digging into your back, legs wrapping around waist!

Your cream filling me once again as those clasping walls convulsing around your phallus, when again my climax envelops body!

Limp like a necklace, hanging around your neck, my body weak in satisfaction!

Purring like a cat, at the thought that I've been taken!

Happiness

I've rarely found happiness in my life.

It's there, then it's gone!

Like being on a ship at sea.

Looking out from the observation deck, at the dolphins breaking water. Seen for a fleeting moment, then disappearing beneath the waves.

Or the whale surfacing only to plunge back into the depths, there for just a moment.

My childhood had no such moments, just one long bout of unhappiness. An only child for ten years, my father abdicating his responsibility and disappeared for some years. My mother a workingwoman in the 1950's.

So I lived with my grandparents. They did there best, but I was a lonely little boy. And so unhappy!

Then came education, well truth be told for reasons too long to go into here, didn't happen. I never went to school for many years, stuck babysitting my mother in Kenya.

While my errant father continued his globetrotting in the guise of work!

Eventually returning home to Blighty they packed me off to "Crown Woods" a three thousand pupil inner London comprehensive school.

As a kid with no formal education, they stuck me in the C stream, with The Bash Street Kids. Another year of extreme unhappiness!

Work fared no better, a few fleeting glimpses of a whale or a dolphin but in general deep unhappiness.

Relationships the same, women have come, women have gone. Mostly leaving awake of unhappiness. Some I have to say in honesty self-inflicted wounds!

The women in my life today, again bring glimpses of a whale or two. But in general, they only bring disappointment to my world! Except for one! Who I'm probably the disappointment!

So one may ask, where do you get your zest for life? Your absolute positivity? Your love for life? Your drive? Your creativity? Your wanton lust for pleasure? Because anyone who knows me will testify its true.

It simple,

I seek Happiness!

Her Picture

It began with that.

His long finger was arrested in its lazy, languid, bored downwards scroll by her image.

A slight intake of breath
An appreciative lift of the eyebrows
A smile
An impossible sense of recognition

He did not know her, but she seemed familiar

He studied her face

The eyes, the mouth, the nose, the cheekbones

He stroked the stubble on his chin and leaned forward slightly in his chair.

With his eyes closed, he imagined her. And he could picture her entirely in his head.

He guided the cursor and clicked the 'fan' button.

Her picture on her profile

It began with that!

Attraction is a mystery

What is it that captures, captivates and compels?

What is it that draws us, like iron to the magnet, bee to honey, moth to light? What is it that makes us warm to another, need to make contact, need to be in their presence, or just make us catch our breath when they come close?

Is it in their eyes, or their mouth? Is it the arc of their smile? Is it in their height, their weight, their curves and lines? Is it in the colour of their skin or their hair? Is it in their laughter, or their voice, or their words, or the intelligent mind within?

Is it in their honesty?
Their truth?
Their empathy?
Their kindness?
Their compassion?
Their hope?

Is it in their movement, their balance, the way their body moves when they walk? Is it in the clothes they wear?

Is it in what they do, what they like, what they believe?

Is it in their beauty, and the beauty they see around them?

Is it about how good they make us feel?

Is it something we instantly see deep in their soul, something we recognise and know? Something that touches our own?

Is it that we sense they will complete us?

Attraction is a mystery.

Even after all these years, I cannot explain it.

But I do know.

I am deeply attracted to you by all of the above.

Dear Friend

You are my friend, and I hope you know that's true.
No matter what happens I will stand by you.

I will be there for you whenever you need.
To lend you a hand or to do a good deed.
So just call on me when you need me, my friend.
I will always be there even to the end.

Beyond

I'm attracted to her not because of her eyes, shining, wide, innocent.

Nor her sculpted cheekbones or the perfect crescent of her smile!

It is not her body, shapely, soft, and elegant.

Nor her breath taking curves or the pure paradise of her silky skin.

It is not her mind, clever, sweet, and eloquent.

Nor her generous heart or her brave, independent soul.

My attraction is something beyond knowing. It's something beyond my understanding.

It's something beyond my control!

Just Once EXPLICIT

If I could taste you

Just once

Your forehead, your cheek, your throat, the nape of your neck

The pulse place just below your ears that you touch with perfume

Your chin, your mouth, your lips, your tongue

Your fingers, your hands, your wrists.

The soft pale inner part of your arm that sees less sun

Your shoulders, your waist, your ribs

The sculpted indentation of your elegant spine

Your breasts, your areola, your hardening nipples

Beautiful and urgent beneath my soft breath

Your toes, your ankles, your shins, your calves

The tender place at the back of your knees

Your thighs, your hips

The perfect peach of your immaculate buttocks

If I could taste you just once

Pressing my lips to your exquisite sex

Letting my tongue glide over your delicate folds

Pressing my mouth to your desire-slick lips

Teasing you with the tip of my tongue

If I could taste you just once

I would lose my appetite for all others!

Sunday Morning

The first day in April, the day and month of my life changing accident those three years ago.

This Sunday morning I walk the beach, the sky is hung blue over the weathered beach huts. A pale sun is smearing the walls with gold. The yellow daffodils are abundant and vivid against green. A magnolia is ripe and creamy with flowers. Birds rustle noisily. The waves crash on golden sands.

There are a million pale green buds bursting open on dark, skeletal trees. Branches and limbs bleed from old scars.

Spring has come. The sap is rising.

I can feel it surging within me too I stride out past Westbeach, along the seafront, past un-open concessions and shifting, silent sand.

I can feel it pulsing through my veins and sense it pumping beneath my skin. I am pleasurably aware of a slight but perceptible tumescence between my thighs.

But it is not the coming summer that is causing my own sap to rise, lifting me in spirit and body on this bold, bright, brave morning.

Unless that summer bears your name!

Even if I wanted to EXPLICIT

I do not dwell on the past.
I cannot bring it back
Even if I wanted to!

It is gone forever. As distant as the outer reaches of
infinite space. As hopeless as waking the dead. As
impossible as immortality.

Nothing I do now can change its nature.
It is set in the hardest of stone. It is unchanging and
permanent. It is fixed and unmoving. Forever.

What value would there be in remembering her? Of
conjuring up sunlit mornings, her breasts cupped in my
hands, nipples hardening against my palms. Her laughter
like music, making me catch her up, and spin her around.

Her eyes bewitching me.

What purpose would there be in recreating her? Of
picturing her dancing in flickering candlelight, her
curves breath taking, her eyes eloquent, her smile only
for me?

Her long, sweet, lingering, hungry, soft, velvet kisses.

I do not dwell on the past

I cannot bring it back.

Even if I wanted to!

Your Back

It has taken me at least a hundred lifetimes to get you out of my system. I have known you forever. Adored you forever. Wanted you forever.

Different names.
Different places.
Different times.

A dozen centuries or more!

Always you.

Your beauty.
Your body.
Your soul.

Winning you.
Owning you.
Then losing you.

And now, is it you?

Are you really back?

I wrote poems for you

Some were bold, burnished, and bright.
They praised your beauty, your body.
Burning for your brilliant mind.

I wrote poems for you.
Some were sweet, silky, and soft.
They were sensual, sexual, and seductive.
Seeking to steal your sacred heart.

I wrote poems for you.
Some were yearning, wanting, craving.
They were aching, thirsting, needing.
Longing to draw you into my arms.

I wrote poems for you.

But they were just wasted unwanted words!

These Days EXPLICIT

When I am alone.

In the sultry, electric heat of a stormy summer
night. In the still, misty air of a hushed and
muted autumn afternoon. In the warm bed contrast of a
shivery bitter-cold winter morning. In the sap-rising new
warmth of a gentle spring evening.

Like this evening, when I am utterly alone

And when my wordy mind is full of dancers. Of
yearning, almost-innocent girls in party dresses. Of
elegant, long-legged women, heels sending staccato
gunfire across marble floors. Of leather-clad vixens, full
of swagger, poise and scarcely admitting vulnerability.
Of submissive, naked angels. Spread and tied like a
sacrifice on pure white sheets on wide brass beds…

And when my memories and fantasies, and the touch
of my own fingers across my flesh, have made me ache
and burn for physical release!

There is always a beauty and a body I conjure up
when I close my eyes.

A delicious smile.
A paradise of curves and lines and soft, tender skin.
A wonder of gorgeous breasts with small soft nipples.
A roll of hips that take my breath away.
A perfection of soft thighs, seductively parted.

Eloquent pale eyes that are getting to know my dark soul.

There is always someone my hunger turns to.

Someone to bring me to a wild, private, exultant, quivering climax!

These days it is always you!

More than I could bear

The church bells are ringing.

Tuesday is the practice night for the faithful and unfaithful campanologists. The peal is uneven, discordant and untidy. A novice is hauling the rope. The sound disturbs the silence. The evenings are usually so quiet here.

I sip my wine. It is nothing special. A Syrah grape without provenance, but it fills my mouth with blackberry, and pepper, and smoke.

And summer.

And memories of her.

She was far too young for me. A child when measured against my white hair and infinite experience. And yet she touched me in a way that few have ever done.

She was lithe and slender and had eyes that saw beyond the obvious, she was as sharp as a glass shard and far more intelligent than she realised. Her demeanour was a mixture of swagger and vulnerability.

She had the face of a model and the bewitching smile of a girl.

She pretended that she was five foot eight, but she wasn't. Her legs were breath taking, her breasts spectacular on such a petite frame.

She was as heavenly as sin.

She gave herself to me with poetic solemnity and a remarkable sense of drama. In retrospect, I think she meant it. She lived for the moment and, just then, with her head bowed, I was the moment.

I am a master of discipline, manipulation and control. But I'm not sure I could ever have tamed her. She was a wild and wayward spirit.

I don't know what has made me think of her. Perhaps the confusion of bells, the wine in my mouth, spring rising, the overwhelming certainty that evening is descending on me fast these days.

We drifted apart.

I am glad we did.

She would have only disappointed me.

And that would have hurt.

More than I could bear.

Primary Objective

On my list, of things to do, you are at the top.

In bold
Underlined
Circled in red
Highlighted
Prioritised
Marked most important
My absolute
My most pressing
My most compelling
Primary objective!

The last thing

The last thing I expected was you!

An impossible creature of bright colours and sunshine, extraordinary beauty, and a perfection of form that takes my breath away.

A profound, vibrant, sensual being.

An unexpected rare, exotic, almost holy gift waiting to be unwrapped.

To be adored and worshipped!

Mirror

In it, she witnesses all her perceived imperfections, all her imagined failings, and all her familiar faults. She has compared herself to others and found herself wanting.

She sees no joy in her own reflection.

I tell her to imagine the glass as my own eyes. To believe that it is I who is admiring her curves, studying her lines, exploring her body, becoming lost in her beauty.

She momentarily catches a glimpse of herself as I see her, her perfection captured in my vision.

She half senses the reason for my adoration.

She almost understands why she thrills me so!

Her Voice.

It was late afternoon in early spring on a sweet and fabled Thursday. The sinking sun was glittering through the trees that surrounded my apartment. The day had been vivid with her distant presence.

It might have been in the past, but it was today.

Her desire could be taut, electric, vibrant, and eloquent. It shivered in her breathing, whispered in her sighs, lifted in hunger as her yearning grew.

My ears were filled with the long ache that carried her relentlessly to an intense, glorious, almost-holy-but-gorgeously-earthly resolution.

I heard her voice.

But it didn't call my name!

Music

I love music

It has been a constant joy throughout my life

And my tastes are catholic

From:
Dirty, raunchy rock
Desperate, yearning, aching blues
Bold and brassy soul
Eloquent, erudite funky jazz,
Opulent, rich, passionate opera
Clever, cool classical
Brave new country
Hypnotic trance
Inspired indie
Vibrant African
Gorgeous Arabic
Magical South American
Fiery, Spanish flamenco
Tortured French chanson
Mournful Portuguese Fado
Earthy English Folk

I love all kinds of music

Most of all

I love music that reminds me of you!

Thinking of you

And hoping you are reading this.

I imagine the light of the screen making your face pale.

Your slight frown of concentration
Your head tilted a little to one side
Your lips parted
Your index finger playing with your hair, curling a silky strand backwards and forwards round and round.

I imagine you scanning the words. Wanting them to be for you. Telling yourself they are not. Yet knowing they can be for no other.

I imagine you glowing, and the faintest blush kissing your skin

I am thinking of you

And hoping you are reading this

And that your perfect mouth is smiling

As I am!

SMS EXPLICIT

Sunday morning sex is lazy and languid
It starts as a slow dance
Mouths touching nipping at lips
His to her neck, hers to his stubbly face

Moving down he's caressing her breasts
As she toys with his hardening cock
His lips on soft mammary flesh then nipple
Her hand on the now hard meat starts a slow beat

His fingers now in the folds of her wet sex
As her mouth sucks at his frenulum
She whispers in his ear
'Assume the position.'

He dutifully does as instructed
Rolling over on to back
She straddles him
Cock in hand she finds her clit

Now slowly she starts
To rub the head against her slit
He moans
His hands now play with her tits

A slow groan slips from her lips
As his shaft she positions
Then she descends
Her body swallowing him whole

The ride begins
She mounted on her stallion
With finger on clit
She rides with passion

The stallion bucks
Fingers wanking her slit
As the horse now beneath her she fucks
He moans, fuck does he moan

As she feels the warm gush inside
The Horse does buck
And throws her on her back
Now rolls reversed

His mouth around her wet spunky slit
His tongue laps at her sexy milk
The tongue finds its mark
And like a dog she does bark

Then it comes in a rush
Her orgasm arrives
It throbs deep
As he sucks it from her body

Then as slowly as it started
They slip back into sleep

Sunday Morning Sex,
a slow dance to start your week!

There is a woman

She walks this earth.

I have not met her, although I once came close. I have barely seen her, though glimpses have thrilled me. I have never spoken to her, although I swear I can hear her sweet accent in my head, and in my dreams.

I do not know her perfume, but her scent thrills me. I have not touched her but can almost feel her skin beneath my fingertips.

I have not looked into her eyes, but feel light-headed at the thought.

I have not held her, but the hunger to do so consumes me.

There is a woman.

She walks this earth!

Naked

Shivering small birds are building a nest above my window.

A fragile, bright, blue-skied day is being threatened by the outriders of an army of clouds.

It is still bitter cold. The uncertain sun has no warmth in it.

This stillborn English spring has frozen the bare trees and scared the bold daffodils shut.

In my warm contemporary apartment, with words and letters of you dripping from my Mont Blanc, I sip from my steaming mug of Assam tea, and I think of you...

Naked!

Spank

They say there is a film called
Fifty Shades of Grey?
So this Valentines Day,
I'd like to lead you astray.

On this day of romance,
come over to my lair?
As an erotic night,
I would like you to share!

Tied with a cord, and a pretty little chain.
And maybe impatient to experience a little pain?

Your senses now ready to be explored.
Your body eager prepared to be adored.

Trusting me, you do not resist.
A strong bond between us does exist.
For your trust in me, I do thee thank.
As your exposed bottom, I start to spank!

The Message

She read the message carefully and, just for the briefest of beats she imagined herself as his lover, his submissive, his muse and his friend.

For a second she held her breath and let the tingle run through her.

For an instant, she saw a wild, intense, and utterly insane affair with him filling her days with something unique, sexual, special, raw and electric.

Something that she knew was once-in-a-lifetime.

But not this lifetime!

Or her lifetime!

She smiled and shook her head.

With a finger full of complete certainty she tapped the delete key.

It was his final message to her.

Beauty

I am no stranger to beauty
It has thrilled me
haunted me
betrayed me
pursued me
evaded me
It has danced wild with me
Through soft, velvet night
It has lain gently with me
In the quiet, silver dawn

I am no stranger to beauty
It has inspired me
Calmed me
Enraged me
Tortured me
Chained me
It has walked comfortably with me
On golden summer days
It has danced only for me
With urgent promise in its eyes

I am no stranger to beauty

But yours …

Brown eyed
And naked
Pale skinned
And perfect
Has taken my breath away!

Men

There are men
who are
young
viral
tattooed
pierced
muscular
famous
and maybe in a Boy Band?

Then there are other men
with money
with power
with violence
with greed and excess.

And then there's me
with just my Mont Blanc
paper and my imagination?

Something for her EXPLICIT

She wishes he would write something for her.

A fantasy of endless, velvet, star-filled skies.

Of a wild, round, luminous moon hanging like a silver lantern. Of a warm, perfumed breeze stroking her hair and tugging gently at her dress.

Of the distant strains of a yearning, lone violin fading and rising through the whispering trees.

Of his hands releasing the pale silk gown from her eloquent shoulders, the dress running off her naked body like a caress and falling with a sigh at her feet.

Of her perfect, dangerous, wondrous curves laid out by him on a cool, crisp white linen sheet. Of her arms and legs stretched wide. Of his tongue, his lips, his fingers over every inch of her tingling skin, upon her sensual mouth, her exquisite breasts, and her urgent, swollen, fragrant sex.

Of him filling her with pleasure, with joy, and with himself.

In every way

She wishes he would write something for her.

The Letter

The little-yellowed envelope
found under loose attic floorboards
beckoned me.

I picked it up, blew away the dust, read the name,
Jack Johnson first owner of this house, now over one
hundred years old.

My hands shook as I drew out the folded letter,
as I slowly opened it, a lock of hair fell to the floor.

A piece of history about to be revealed, typed on a
single sheet, and dated June 20, 1900.

'My Dearest Jack,' it began.
'I sit naked before my typewriter, searching for words
and the keys to put them on paper.'

I felt I had invaded this couple's privacy,
a voyeur of an event that had happened
over a century ago.

My curiosity was aroused, I continued to read.

'I have missed you so since our last meeting......it was
all too brief.
You have taught me about my body, allowed me to
unleash my passion, and excited me beyond my wildest
imagination.'

'Now we are apart.........I sit here naked, no longer a virgin, longing for your kiss.

My body cries out for your tender touch.
I would give myself to you freely, opening myself to you once more, if but for one night.'

There was no signature, only the words, 'Sealed with a kiss,' and the impression of the writer's lips.

I carefully refolded the paper around the lock of hair, slid it back into the envelope, and returned it to its dusty resting place under the floorboards.

I have often wondered if they ever did meet again.

I hope they had.

She is attracted to him

And she is afraid of him.

Not because of how he looks. She has no idea of his appearance except for the almost cryptic description in his online profile. She conjures up a tall, slender, elegant, middle-aged man, with silver hair and eyes that either dance with laughter or brood black as night. But she could be wrong.

She has heard his voice. An ordinary Englishman with excellent diction and a slightly over-theatrical delivery when he reads.

It thrills her. And chills her, but she does not know why.

But is it the words themselves that compel her and disturb her. Not because they are particularly smart or literary or wise or beautiful. He has described himself as a word juggler, and she half agrees with him. Smoke and mirrors. Conjuring tricks with adjectives and verbs.

No. It is not his style but the content itself that touches her.

She is attracted to him

And she is afraid of him

Because he speaks directly to her heart!

Friends

The old man turned to me and asked,
'How many friends have you?'
Why 10 or 20 friends have I,
And named off just a few.

He rose quite slowly with effort,
and sadly shook his head.
'A lucky child you are,
to have so many friends,' he said.

But think of what you're saying,
there is so much you do not know.
A friend is just not someone
to whom you say 'Hello.'

A friends a tender shoulder
on which to softly cry.
A well to pour your troubles down
and raise your spirits high.

A friend is a hand to pull you up
from darkness and despair.
When all your other 'so-called' friends
have helped to put you there.

A true friend is an ally
who can't be moved or bought.
A voice to keep your name alive
when others have forgot.

But most of all a friend is a heart
a strong and sturdy wall.
For from the hearts of friends
there comes the greatest love of all.

So think of what I've spoken
for every word is true.
And answer once again my child
how many friends have you!

Once

Once in a lifetime
You will find someone
Who touches not only your heart
But also your soul

Once in a lifetime
You will discover someone
Who stands beside you
Not over you

Once in a lifetime
You will find someone
Who loves you for who you are
And not for what you are or could be

Once in a lifetime
If you're lucky
You find that someone
As I found you!

After the rain the flowers bloom

When your life seems as bleak as the darkest night.
And you just want your troubles to up and take flight.
When your emotions are drained.
Or you're full of pain.
And the tears pour out, just like the rain.

When your life appears to be falling apart.
And nothing can aid your aching heart.
God in his wisdom sent me you.
A shoulder to cry on, to help me through.

An angel to stand by my side.
Someone in whom I can confide.
For at the end of the tunnel there is a light.
A hand to guide me in my plight.

For out of the darkness shines the moon.
And after the rain the flowers bloom.
Now my life is full of zest.
For I surely am the one that's blessed.

Inch by Inch

I am the poetic cartographer

of your sacred body.

I will discover you

and map you,

explore you

and draw you,

observe you

and describe you,

chart you

and render you

inch by perfect inch!

My Path

I have reached a point in my life

through trial and error

joy and sorrow

hope and regret

tears and laughter

pain and pleasure

love and guilt

where I know

what is right

for me.

I walk my own path!

The door to my heart

I am a sensitive soul.

Perhaps too much for a man.

I sigh at beauty. I am enchanted by charm. I can get lost in a look.

I cry at sad movies, often glad of the dark.

I am a romantic, sad songs in my earbuds. Black and white films in the winter. Meetings in steamy-window bookshop cafes. Walks by the swan-gliding river. Dinner in the flickering light of whispering candles.

A message on my phone that ends in a kiss.

I am a dreamer. A poet. Someone who will never forget the press of her lips.

And sometimes, only sometimes, I am a fool.

Yet for all that above, if I am hurt, I can become as hard and as cold as a Siberian frost.

And the door to my heart

Slams

Shut!

Something

There is something

about you

a quality

an intelligence

a wit

a generosity of spirit

even more compelling

even more adorable

even more desirable

than the exquisite beauty

of your bone and muscle

and of your hair and skin.

There is defiantly something about you!

First Sighting

I remember

the first time

I saw you

I raised an eyebrow

shook my head

sighed

smiled

sipped my wine

and inwardly applauded

in sincere and silent

admiration!

Ink

I have a beautiful

elegant silver

Mont Blanc

fountain pen.

I imagine

writing my name

on your exquisite

perfect skin.

In dark

Midnight Blue

Ink!

Rare Creature

She is a rare creature

she makes me write

she makes me sing

she makes me high.

She makes me dance

she makes me ache

she makes me sigh.

She makes me believe

she makes me wish

she makes me try.

And sometimes all these things at the same time!

Instant Addiction

You are that

utterly intoxicating

completely breath-taking

totally electrifying

first try

single fix

immediate hit

raw rush

heavenly high

instant addiction

I never knew

existed!

Sleeping Beauty EXPLICIT

She is sleeping

Her breathing is shallow. Her chest rises and falls. He counts the seconds and studies her for signs of waking.

There are none.

He says her name.

Softly.

Again.

A little louder.

But still quietly.

He does not really want her to stir.

He gently takes her hand in his. It is small, and soft, and cool. Her fingers lie over his. They are quiet and still. His thumb and forefinger circle her wrist. He can feel her pulse. He imagines it quickening, but he cannot be sure. He lowers her hand to the bed.

She is beautiful. Her hair is raven black against her pale skin. Her lips are perfectly formed and ruby-red. She is wearing a pure white dress that is fitted at the breast, tight at the waist, and clinging to her hips.

A Sleeping Beauty

He knows he should kiss her, rousing her from her slumber, bring her back to consciousness.

But her still and perfect form has mesmerised him, captivated him, and bewitched him. He feels himself harden as he moves towards her. He murmurs her name again. His throat stifles the sound.

He reaches out, and with almost trembling fingers he strokes her cheek. Her skin is warm to his touch.

She does not stir.

He carefully undoes the first of the buttons.

And then another.

And a third.

The gorgeous swell of her breasts makes him dizzy with desire.

At the sixth button, as the material begins to peel open, he realises she is naked underneath!

....

She is not sleeping.

She senses him standing by the narrow bed, gazing at her. She knows his eyes are upon her, taking in every curve, and every line. She waits. And tries to control her breathing.

She focuses on keeping perfectly still.

She hears him say her name.

Twice.

She ignores it, forbidding her eyelids to flicker.

He picks up her hand. His unexpected touch in the darkness almost makes her flinch with surprise. His fingers are long and thin. She fears he will feel her pulse racing crazily as his thumb pressed against her flesh. He releases her gently, and she knows.

She is sure about what is going to happen when she hears her name a third time, and it is said like a faint prayer in a hoarse and caressing whisper.

His touch upon her cheek is like fire. She almost gasps at her own arousal.

He begins to undo the buttons of her dress.

Achingly.

Tantalizingly.

Deliciously slowly.

This is heaven.

She will not wake now!

Printed in Great Britain
by Amazon

66432706R00090